Get Things Done with Trello

Your Quick Access to Productivity and Success includes a Step-by-Step Guide to Set Up and Implement Trello

Dominic Wolff

ORGANIZED LIVING
P R E S S

Atlanta, Georgia USA

ISBN 978-1-50043-798-5

9 781500 437985 >

EDITORIAL REVIEWS

I thought I was a hopeless cause when it came to organizing. TRELLO GTD certainly helped me sort things and gave me a clear picture of what's really important. Lifesaver!

- Stacey Peters, Portland, OR

I used to think making lists were boring. But thanks to the book, I changed perspectives. I now have a list for pretty much every aspect in my life.

- Jacqueline Hall, Sedalia, MO

Trying to remember the things from my mental to-do list used to be a problem. I don't have that issue anymore ever since I started using the TRELLO GTD system. I highly recommend this book to all the busy bees out there.

- Rachel Burns, Ross, ND

Thank you for downloading my book. Please REVIEW this book on Amazon. I need your feedback to make the next version better. Thank you so much!

BOOKS BY DOMINIC WOLFF

Master Getting Things Done the David Allen Way with Evernote

Getting Things Done (GTD) + Evernote = Ultimate Productivity

Total Time Mastery with Evernote

Your Killer Linkedin Profile

Building Connections 2014

Time Management Mastery

Speak Up!

How to Get Things Done with OneNote

FOREWORD

I remember a time when productivity was the least of my worries. I would just do anything that came to mind and move on to the next task. But as I became an adult, my responsibilities started to grow too. I couldn't remember tasks on top of my head any longer because there were too many of them. Writing them down in lists was the best way to go about it.

That's what Dominic Wolff advocates in his book on the TRELLO GTD system. In order for you to accomplish your tasks and projects, you need to write them down and just do it. Just do it and get it over with. It's pretty basic but it's also very effective. When tasks related to your goals are laid out in front of you, you have to act on them.

Aside from organizing your daily responsibilities, Wolff also teaches how you can materialize your dreams by breaking them down into small tasks. When you are acting on these small tasks, you are slowly making your dreams a reality. Imagine if you could also do this for your other big goals. Who knows how far you can go when you apply the TRELLO GTD principle in your life.

TABLE OF CONTENTS

1

Introduction

Imagine waking up on your regular day. You step into the shower and discern about the things you need to do: pick up work clothes at the dry cleaners, submit a final proposal to boss, buy cat food at the store, get x-ray results from the clinic. You reckon today is going to be a busy day. There are so many things to do. Despite this, you don't bother to write the tasks down as you're busy getting dressed for work. You feel confident you'll remember the tasks as the day goes by.

After a long hard day at work, you immediately go home and grab a tub of ice cream to cope with the stress. Other tasks can wait. As you finish your last scoop of ice cream and the TV series you're watching, you tell yourself, "Just one more episode." You fall asleep in front of the television without noticing. The next thing you know, it's already another day and you have to get ready for work again. You go to the closet to change only to find nothing decent to wear because you failed to pick up your office clothes at the dry cleaners yesterday. The cat suddenly meows loud like a bawling baby waiting to be fed. This reminds you that you also forgot to buy cat food yesterday.

You end up arriving at work three hours late because you had to buy cat food and pick up your work clothes at the dry cleaners. The boss yells at you and complains about your tardiness and idleness. Gossipy colleagues outside can hear who the boss is scolding at and for what. You wish to just disappear right there to make this all end. All this happens simply because you forgot to do yesterday's tasks.

Believe it or not, this kind of chaos is what most people are accustomed to. As soon as they wake up, they swear to start a brand new day of efficiency and productivity. They make a mental to-do list only to forget it, remember it later, and realize it's already a day or a week late.

This is not a good way to live but unfortunately, many people do. In this book, I will help you organize your tasks and increase your productivity with the help of two key tools. As a business owner, I see time as a very valuable asset. You know the saying, "Life is too short." I believe that every second of the day should be maximized. I'm always on the lookout for new ways to use my time more efficiently.

I believe my interest in business and productivity started when I was a kid. I would sell candy bars hoping to gain profit. I would then buy and sell more candy bars to increase my profit even more. I've gone a long way since then. Today, I run a multi-state company and I frequently write articles for business publications.

Being in the business world has taught me many things. I've developed the habit of managing my tasks and using my time wisely. Every day is a never-ending quest to become more productive. I find that when my tasks are in order, I have more time to do other things.

4

I can spend time with my family and I get to enjoy my hobbies. It's amazing how much time you free up when you just manage your time responsibly. In my case, I always make sure to keep a pen and paper handy. I want to be ready to write something down in case an idea comes out of nowhere. You never know when inspiration strikes. I then transfer these listed ideas to my TRELLO board. If you're wondering what TRELLO is, it's a great task management tool that has helped me get my busy life together. I don't just limit using TRELLO to just ideas. I also plan my goals, business objectives and chores around TRELLO. Later, you will understand why I can't stop raving about this tool.

Despite productivity tools like TRELLO being easily accessible to busy people like us, many still find themselves saying these things:

"I'm busy."

"I have a lot of things to do."

"I wish there were more than 24 hours in a day."

"I'm sorry, but my calendar is fully booked."

These phrases might sound familiar to you. You may have heard a friend, family or a colleague utter these phrases at one time. In the times that we live in, it's no surprise to hear these from people. I even find myself saying these things once in a while. But why is that? This is the digital age. Everything is supposed to be easier. Shopping, paying bills, and ordering food used to be tasks that would require you to get out of the house. Now you don't have to since you can do all of them online. You can record your favorite TV shows. You can even get an update on traffic using an app. Almost everything can be done in an instant!

So what seems to be the problem? People seem busier than ever despite technological advancement's ability to make the most daunting tasks easy. I believe there are two reasons why people still feel so strapped for time. It's because 1) when tasks are not externalized, they seem undoable and 2) this generation has a whole new set of distractions.

It wouldn't be fair to say that distractions can easily be eliminated by turning the TV off or going to a quiet place. Today's distractions are much different compared to those of decades ago. They come in the form of frequent notifications from social media, emails, or a funny video you found on your newsfeed. These things seem harmless at a glance. Some people even deny they get distracted by them. But when you consider the frequency of these little distractions and the hours they add up to, you get a bigger picture of how much time you're actually wasting.

For example, your habit of checking social media 10 times a day for 10 minutes actually adds up to 100 minutes. That's 500 hours equivalent to 8.3 hours of wasted time in a 40-hour work in a week. It's safe to say that you just wasted more than one day of work just to check social media. This amount of time could have been better spent accomplishing tasks that bring you closer to your goals. Although a little distraction is good for stress relief, too much of it can kill productivity.

As promised earlier, I'm going to teach you how to avoid killing your productivity with the help of two tools: GTD and TRELLO. With the TRELLO tool and GTD method, you'll avoid wasting time on small distractions and focus on the small tasks that bring you one step closer to your goals. By the time you finish reading this book, you will learn how to live a productive life where there's order, tangible goals, and more free time to do the things you like.

I know you must be wondering how we're going to make all of this possible so let us go ahead and start.

Getting Started With GTD

What is GTD?

GTD, or Getting Things Done, is a method of organizing and tracking tasks founded by personal productivity expert David Allen. He wrote the National Bestseller book *Getting Things Done: The Art of Stress-Free Productivity* and his work has been recognized in highly respected publications like Fast Company, Fortune, The Los Angeles Times, The New York Times and The Wall Street Journal.

The GTD system has helped many people bring order into their chaotic lives. Vague goals turn into actionable tasks which result in less stressful and more manageable life. GTD helps free the brain of space for more productive thinking. You can create fresh and new ideas since your mind is not congested with a giant list of things to do. Instead of keeping a mental to-do list, the GTD system promotes using physical notes and productivity tools that help you in getting your thoughts in order.

:anding how **GTD Works**

The GTD method is very easy to implement. Below are the five principles you need to remember when using GTD.

1. Capture

   This is similar to brainstorming, except that with GTD, you are required to write down and record the tasks, errands, projects and things to finish. Write everything that comes to mind. Use any tool that will allow you to go back to the list later. It can be a smartphone, a computer, a pen and paper or a voice recorder. Anything that is convenient for you.

2. Clarify

   After writing everything down, it's time to ask the question: Is this task actionable? Use this query for each task and throw it in the trash if the answer is no. If yes, write down the next action needed to accomplish the task. This helps shorten your list to avoid tasks that are vague and unimportant.

3. Organize

   Organize your list by category. Looking at an extensive list of uncategorized tasks can be very daunting. By categorizing your list, everything looks manageable since all items are placed at a list where they need to be.

   For example, you can make separate lists for groceries, emails to send, calls to make and topics to write. You'll also know which list is appropriate for a certain situation. When you're checking your email, you know you need to look at the "Emails to send" list. If you're at the groceries, just carry the "Grocery list" with you.

4. Reflect

   Review your lists regularly and determine what you need to do next. The GTD system works best when you constantly check up on your tasks. You can do a weekly review to crash out accomplished tasks and add new ones on the list. This also gives you the chance to remove pending tasks which you deem are not worth accomplishing.

5. Engage
   Don't get distracted. Take a look at your list and just do the tasks that appear on it. The fact that your tasks are actionable makes them much easier to tackle.

CCORE, which stands for Capture, Clarify, Organize, Review and Engage, is very easy to remember. By definition, the word 'core' means the most essential part of something. Remember that in order to achieve your goals in life, you need to get the essential things done. Develop the discipline to follow the principles above and you'll find yourself succeeding in things you thought were impossible.

Benefits of Using GTD

There are plenty of benefits to gain from applying the GTD system in your daily life. In my case, I get to spend time with my wife and children. Thanks to GTD. When using the GTD method, you will get the list of the benefits below:

- You gain a feeling of relaxed control

Most people get stressed out from feeling as if they don't have control over their lives. They feel trapped and they surrender to the idea that their circumstances will never change. This doesn't have to be the case. When you apply the GTD method, you free your mind from mental notes and organize them in a reliable external system. When goals and ideas are written and broken down into small actionable steps, you will gain a sense of control and eliminate stress and anxiety caused by poor self-organization.

- It keeps you on track

GTD allows you to check on your life constantly. Part of the GTD principles is to review your notes. When you review on a weekly basis, you can see the status of your projects. Goals are easy to track. You'll know how much you still have to do just by looking at the unaccomplished tasks that fall under a goal. Evaluate which tasks are important and eliminate those which are not. When you lose track, you can always get back by adding, deleting, and modifying tasks that will bring you to the right direction.

- You have the freedom to choose

GTD is a system that does not dictate how you should do your tasks. You have the freedom to choose what you want and don't want to do. You won't get penalized for not doing a task, although you are responsible for the consequences that come if a task goes unfinished for too long. This is why discipline is so important when using GTD. Your intuition is in charge and it is in your best judgment which tasks should be prioritized.

- Consistency in making and keeping commitments

Constantly breaking commitments can hurt relationships. Imagine waiting for a friend at a restaurant. He calls to tell you he can't make it because he just woke up and he's not in the mood to go out. How would you feel? Upset? Angry? Rejected? Those are just some of the feelings people have when you don't commit to an established schedule.

With GTD, never again will you forget that gift you promised your niece or that friend's birthday party you swore to attend. GTD tracks your commitments and helps you accomplish them in a timely manner. Of course, there will be commitments that are not as important. Utilize GTD by assigning priority levels to different commitments.

- It regains your focus

Since everything is captured in your notes and tools like TRELLO, your mind is free from distractions. You can focus on the task at hand and finish it knowing that it's recorded in your notes. Crashing out a finished task from your list will leave you feeling fulfilled. This will make you want to tackle more projects just to have that feeling again.

- Track your dreams

Got a dream that seems intangible like "be a successful public speaker" or "own a business someday"? When stated, these goals seem impossible to achieve. They sound too huge to tackle. With

GTD, you create small tangible tasks that will lead you to the fulfillment of your dream. The reason why some people settle for small goals is because their dreams seem too big to handle.

All you actually need to do is set up small actionable tasks and just act on them. The next thing you know, you're already sitting on top of your success. It may seem like a tedious process, but a slow but sure pace has proved to benefit plenty of people.

- Unleashes the creative side in you

When the mind is free of worries, you allow yourself to generate more thoughts and ideas. Let your imagination run free. You can try to invent a new product or implement a process that's never been tried before. With GTD, you have a wider space to be creative.

- Better organization

This is one of the main purposes of the GTD method. For those who seek a solution to a chaotic life of unfinished tasks, missed deadlines and late appointments, GTD is the answer. GTD forces you to be organized as you list down everything you need to do and arrange them by category. One for groceries, movies to watch, articles to write, etc. You get to feel calm knowing that everything is in place.

- Stimulates advanced thinking

Results are expected with each task. GTD keeps you from overanalyzing goals and lets you focus on the task at hand since the thinking and planning has already been dealt with in advance. You don't let your work define you, but instead, you define your work.

- Manage uncertainty better

Times are uncertain. New challenges and opportunities come to you every day. Your plans and priorities are flexible with GTD. When something new comes up, you can always refer to your list and make the appropriate changes.

- Increased productivity

Being able to track your dreams, check your projects, keep commitments, and think in advance will help you become an overall productive person. It's just simply the result from using the GTD method.

There are plenty of benefits to enjoy for a method that is as simple as GTD. It's easy to implement and if you are really serious about being better at time management, you will eventually reap the results. You just have to make sure all your tasks are written down and organized. Above all, you must have the discipline to act on them.

The Basics of TRELLO

By now, you must be wondering what tool we will use to track down these tasks. I understand everyone's to-do lists greatly vary which would explain why everyone uses different productivity tools. I've already introduced TRELLO to you earlier. In this chapter, I will tell you what you need to know about this tool. Knowing that TRELLO is a tool fully capable of organizing all types of tasks, projects and plans, it will not take much convincing for you to switch to it. TRELLO is a flexible tool that you can take advantage of whether you're using it for business, school or work. Throw away your calendars and thick organizers because in the next chapters, I'll teach you how to use the only tool you will ever need to get your life together.

TRELLO is a collaboration tool you can use to help organize projects and tasks into boards. It helps get things done on time, whether you are working solo or with a group. You can keep multiple boards, create checklists and work with other members in real time. The tool has been already great as it is but be ready for more amazing features as the website developers are seeking new ways to enhance TRELLO.

At the moment, iPhone and Android support TRELLO.

17

However, the website is designed to be accessible to most mobile devices. An iPad application was recently released last March 12, 2013.

I find TRELLO a wonderful productivity tool after using it for quite some time. I'm sure you will have the same sentiments too if you use it yourself. I like the fact that it lets you break down tasks into small actionable steps. It really lets you get to the specifics. You can even go as far as making a checklist for your list. This greatly helps in making an overwhelming project seem less daunting.

I use TRELLO mostly for my business where I create separate boards for new projects. But sometimes, one board for one project is not enough. If a project is too big, I create an organization with its own set of boards that cover the different areas of the project. I also use TRELLO for travel where I can organize my things such as the luggage, plane tickets and itinerary. When I sort these tasks with TRELLO, I'm less stressed and I enjoy the trip more.

I know you are excited to use TRELLO but before we do, I want to get down to the basic features first. It's important to know the features before using it and implementing the GTD method.

TRELLO 101: Features and Benefits

So how does a typical TRELLO board look like? Imagine a huge bulletin board with lists arranged in columns. Each column can represent different things depending on the kind of project you're working on. The lists have cards attached to them. On each card, you can make even more lists called checklists.

You can create as many boards, lists and cards as needed. When you create a new board in TRELLO, you will typically get the three default lists named "To Do," "Doing" and "Done." Here's an example of how the board looks like when the lists are filled with tasks.

When you're using TRELLO, just a quick glimpse of it will already give you detailed information about your project from which include tasks being worked on, the names of the members working on a task, and the nature of a certain task. Once you're done with a task, just move it to the appropriate list. It will give you a clear picture of where you stand with your responsibilities.

Features

TRELLO has many features, many of which will be tackled more in the later chapters of the book. Now, we'll just discuss the main features considered as the three hierarchal levels of information: **boards, lists and cards.**

1. TRELLO Boards

All projects that you create will be organized into boards. Adding members allows you to collaborate with other people on a project. You get to see a full picture of the project without having to be in the same room with your team members. If you are not the administrator of a board, you can either be invited or add yourself as a member. Depending on the project's size, you can create as many boards and invite as many members as you want.

On the lower right hand corner of the page are the Menu, Add Members option, and the activity feed where you can see the updates of activities on the board.

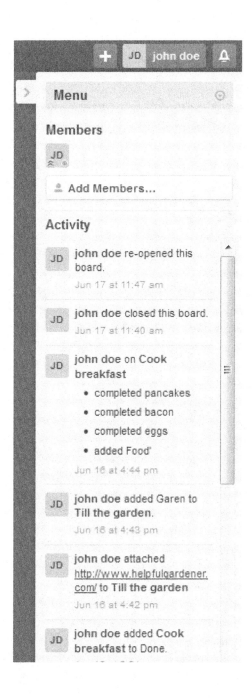

The feed is updated in real time with the last few events and you will see what the other members are doing on the board as well. If you need to see more activities, you can expand the list by clicking View All. This lets you view activities from the time that you created the board.

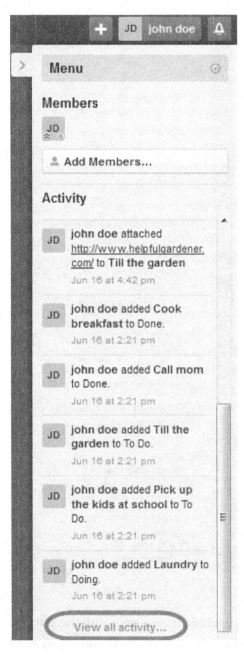

2. TRELLO Lists

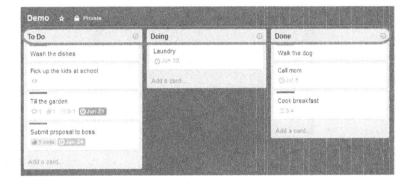

Lists are the columns arranged on the board. You can customize the title for each list and add as many as you need. Your strategy to naming lists will depend on you. It can be by team member, by project stage, or by subject. It really depends on which works best for you and your team. List titles give direction to the user about the flow of work involved on a board.

3. TRELLO Cards

Cards give detailed information about what needs to be done on a specific list. You can create numerous cards for each list depending on how many tasks fall under that list. They can easily be moved from one list to another just by dragging.

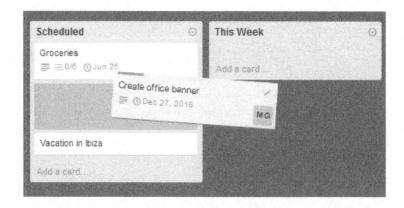

The cards hold the most information than any other unit in the board and each one can have the following sections:

a. The **title** briefly explains what the card is for.
b. The **comment area** is where users can comment about the activity involved.
c. **Add/remove** option is where new members for a particular card can be added.
d. File **attachment** option allows you to grab files from your Mac or PC.
e. **Subscribe** button is where a user can subscribe to a card. This notifies them of a card's activity without the need for the user to be a member of the card.
f. The **checklist** contains the list of items to be checked off. Once a task is completed, you can check off the item and the completion bar will move in percentage format to show the progress you've made.
g. The **due date** is to indicate and inform the members of the deadline for a specified task.

Earlier, I have mentioned that aside from boards, you can also create organizations. Though it's a feature that I rarely use, I highly recommend it when you are handling large-scale projects. You can experiment with organizations later as soon as you master manipulating the TRELLO's features.

Benefits

Aside from helping you organize your thoughts into boards and small lists, there are also other benefits to using TRELLO. Below are some of the advantages you will enjoy when you use TRELLO.

- *Easy to use.* Pretty much anyone can use TRELLO. Unlike other project management systems which are too complex, TRELLO is great for any type of workflow. It can be used for business-related projects or as a personal management application.

After you sign up for the service, you will see a Welcome board with lists and cards that has instructions attached to each. By clicking on each card, you will learn more about TRELLO's features such as attaching files, adding hyperlinks and inviting users. Below is how the board looks like if you click on the Welcome board list.

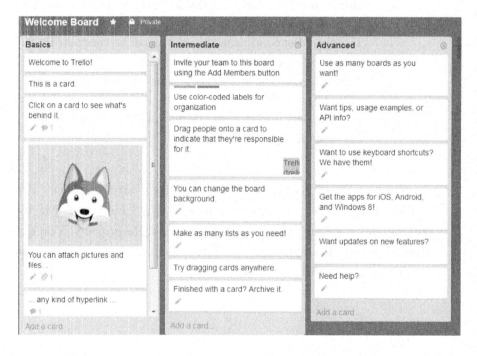

The first board shows you the basic functions. If you want to go a level higher, the second list shows you intermediate ways to use TRELLO like changing the board background and archiving a card. For the advanced, refer to the third list where you will learn how to navigate TRELLO with keyboard shortcuts and learn about the API.

- *Encourages collaboration and accountability.* With TRELLO, you can invite as many people as you want. Once your team is signed up for TRELLO and become members of the board, they will have the same capability like adding cards, making checklists and uploading attachments. TRELLO also makes it easy to let the other members know about the project's status since the activity feed updates real-time and you don't have to click on the refresh button every time.

    You can get an idea of what everyone is doing just by looking at the real-time updates. If you're not on TRELLO all the time, email notifications are available to keep you informed of the latest changes. For tasks you care about the most, you can also get timely updates by subscribing to specific tasks.

- *Security, accessibility and flexibility.* The TRELLO website can be accessed whatever the size of your device may be. All the information is backed up; you don't have to worry about losing information. Your data is private and secure and you can always adjust the privacy options depending on your preference.

    If you want to check on an old task you've already archived, just go to the search bar, type the keyword and it will do all the finding for you. TRELLO can also be used for practically anything: planning a wedding, doing the groceries, choosing a home. You name it.

- *Free and eco-friendly.* There are project management tools out there with similar features as TRELLO but most of them are not for free. With TRELLO, you can enjoy all the wonderful features without having to pay for anything. Organizing projects and managing your projects do not have to be costly. You also save money on paper since you do not have to write all of your tasks down. They can all be recorded using TRELLO.

How to use TRELLO

For starters, you need to create a board. By clicking on the + sign found on the upper right hand corner of the board, you can choose to either add a new board or a new organization. For now, we only need to create a board.

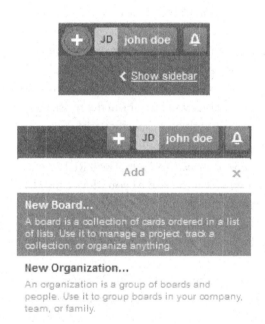

Once you create a new board, you need to make basic lists. The default lists you get when you create a new board are "To do," "Doing," and "Done". You can then start manipulating the lists by writing down your tasks for the day. When you're currently working on one, move the task to the "Doing" list. When you're done, just drag the card to the "Done" list. See how many tasks you can get done in a day. Don't forget to play around with the options. It's a great way to master the tool. As you get better, you can move on to taking advantage of the advanced options.

Once you are used to doing tasks and moving the cards from one column to another, you can move on to using more complex titles for your lists such as "Planning," "In progress," and "Deployment ready." It's up to you what titles you wish to use. Just make sure that it appropriately fits the nature of your project.

For example, if you're a student, you might need to arrange your lists by subject or by week. Or if you have a startup, having a list for each member is a great idea as it allows them to have a clear view of what their assignments are. Don't worry because later in the book, I will teach you how to create boards for different contexts like school, work and business.

If you are working on a project with a group of people, just click on the Add Members button.

TRELLO will automatically prompt users to sign up if a member is not enrolled for the service yet. After enrollment, they will be able to view the board. As members, they too can make changes on the board and their actions will also be tracked and reflected on the feed.

You can also add members to specific cards. This is great when you're designating tasks to different members. On each card, members can put labels, make a checklist, set a due date and attach files.

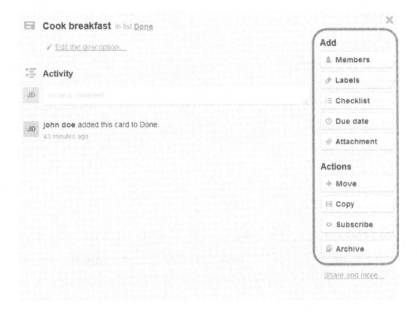

Once a task is done, you can either delete it or archive it. To be on the safe side, I highly recommend that you archive everything in case you need to refer to it later in the future.

Below is an example of the task I created along with the details that will help me in accomplishing it. I named it "Cook Breakfast." Cooking breakfast doesn't have to be this detailed but I just wanted to show you that TRELLO can be applied to almost everything and that it's very detailed. It even has an update feed on the card itself.

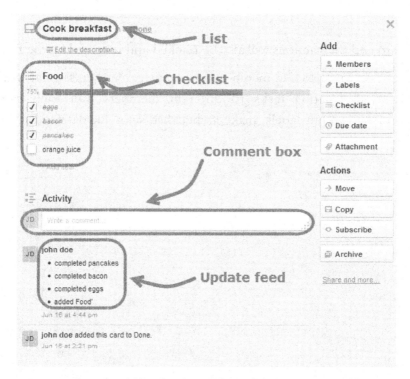

I created a checklist for breakfast which has the names of the foods I'll be cooking. In order for me to accomplish the "Cook breakfast" task, I will have to complete preparing all the meals on the checklist. Every time you mark a check in the box, you'll see a percentage change in progress exhibited by the blue bar. You can also click on the comment box to write a comment on the task.

The figure above is just a basic way to use TRELLO. TRELLO is a pretty intuitive tool so you will know how to manipulate the features right away as soon as you click on them. Once you have gotten used to the basics, you can ante up by using the more advanced features.

Solutions to Common Problems When Using TRELLO

TRELLO is very simple to use, but sometimes, you will encounter issues you might not be familiar with. Below are common issues when using TRELLO and the solutions to each one.

Problem #1: Difficult to do time-tracking

Solution: Use Board Trail. It's an app that allows you to track the duration a card has been on a list. For example, when you're about to start working on a task, just drag the card to the list specified for the project and Board Trail will monitor the duration of the time the card is on the list. When you're done with the task, just drag it back to the "Done" or back to the "To Do" column. At this point, the timer will stop monitoring the task. It's up to you which list on the board you wish to drag the card to. Board Trail will do its job of monitoring the time a card spends on a list.

Problem #2: You're not getting email notifications in a timely manner.

Solution: By default, TRELLO will periodically email you with notifications you haven't dismissed on the web interface. You can modify your email notifications by going to *https://Trello.com/my/notifications* and then adjust your settings at the top of the page.

Problem #3: Push notifications on mobile.

Solution: Push notifications are only available for messages and comments on cards of which you are a member of or subscribed to. Push notifications for due dates are currently not supported on mobile yet.

Problem #4: No option to enable desktop notifications

Solution: This might be due to you previously denying desktop notifications in Chrome, Firefox, or Safari, which might result in not seeing the option to enable desktop notifications in the TRELLO settings page.

You can still change this by modifying the browser settings. If you're using Chrome or Firefox, you can enable desktop notifications by selecting on the lock icon in your browser's address bar. Under Permissions, change the Notifications permissions to allow. For Safari, just select Safari from the browser's header. Go to Preferences, then Notifications and make sure Trello.com is in the list of websites and select Allow.

Problem #5: Due date notifications

Solution: To receive due date notifications, you need to subscribe to the entire board. If you set a due date on a card you are a member of or subscribed to, you will receive a notification about the card 24 hours before it's due.

Problem #6: Importing date into TRELLO

Solution: At the moment, TRELLO does not have an import tool yet, but there are several options to help you bring your data to TRELLO.

a. *Copy and paste* – when you paste a text into a TRELLO card, each new line becomes a new card. For example, if you have a list of card titles in your Excel spreadsheet, just copy the title from one column and each cell of the sheet will become a card with a TRELLO list.

b. *TRELLO API* – this allows you to have a full programmatic control of the import process

c. *Zapier* – a third party tool that lets you integrate other services with TRELLO so if you're using Google spreadsheets, for example, each line in the spreadsheet will be added as TRELLO cards.

If you have too much text, the copy and paste method might be too tedious. You can try using AutoHotKey, which allows you to write scripts that automate PC applications.

Make sure to refer to the list above whenever you encounter any of these issues. The great thing about TRELLO is that almost everything in it is reversible. You can always make corrections when you commit a mistake. The longer you use TRELLO, the more you will get used to it. You might even come up with your own set of advanced techniques that you can share to your fellow TRELLO users.

Managing Tasks Effectively with TRELLO

Now that you're familiar with TRELLO and know how to handle difficult issues, it's time to put it to the test. You can manage tasks effectively with this tool and below are a few tips on how you can do just that:

- Always set a deadline for each task. This defines how much time is needed for each work to be done.

- Subscribe to cards that you want to supervise directly.

- Use the comment section to add more details about a card. You may also use this area as space for your feedback on a certain task. For each comment, you can click on the Mention Member option found below the comment box or just type @ and the name of the member you wish to get attention from.

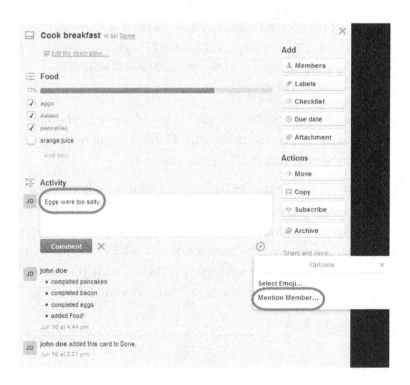

Frequently Asked Questions about TRELLO

Since we're discussing productivity, I want to make sure you don't waste your time looking through forums for answers to questions that have already been asked a million times by TRELLO beginners. This section is dedicated to the frequently asked questions about TRELLO. Below each question are the answers.

What are the main features of TRELLO?

TRELLO allows you to manage your tasks and collaborate with different users in real time using boards, lists and cards. You can invite as many members as you want to the board and you can check recent activity of members on the feed located on the bottom right part of the board. TRELLO works at any screen size. It doesn't matter whether you are using a large desktop computer or a small mobile device, you can still access the website. When you need to look for something on the board, you just have to type in the keyword in the search bar. You can attach photos, drawings and sketches and you don't have to worry about privacy because all data in TRELLO are secure.

How much does TRELLO cost?

TRELLO is free, but you will need to pay if you want to upgrade your TRELLO to enjoy advanced additional features like stickers, board backgrounds, and larger attachments. You only have to pay as low as $5 to enjoy the upgrade features every month. $45 if you want it the whole year. You can even get it for free if you share TRELLO just by inviting new members. Every member you can convince to join gives you a free month to enjoy TRELLO gold. If you can let 12 people join, you can get it for free up to 12 months.

Who are the typical users of TRELLO?

It's typically the freelancers, large enterprises, small and mid-size businesses and non-profits who use TRELLO.

What language does TRELLO support?

At the moment, TRELLO only supports English, but the developers are currently working on its internationalization. You can visit the TRELLO development board and under the In Progress list, look for the card titled TRELLO Internalization/Localization and cast your vote by clicking on the Vote button found on the left hand corner of the card. Under the comment section, you can type in the language you wish TRELLO to be available in.

What's the difference between deleting and archiving a card?

Deleting moves a card to the Trash while Archiving just stores the file in Archived Items folder where you can refer to it later when you need to. Normally, before you can delete a card, you have to archive it first. Once you have archived the item, just go the Menu, click on Archived Items and click on the Delete button.

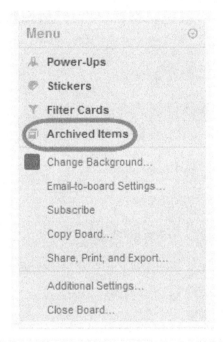

Can I get back a deleted board?

Yes, you can. Just get the board back by selecting the Boards menu and then "See Closed Boards." You will then a see a list of closed boards. On the right side, just click on the reopen button aligned with the board you wish to open.

Closed Boards

Demo

Re-open

You have to have been a board admin to re-open a closed board.

Meal Planning

Is there an upload limit?

Yes. It's 10MB per file.

What are TRELLO's visibility options?

Board administrators can set the board's visibility by clicking on Settings in the board's Menu, then clicking "Change Visibility."

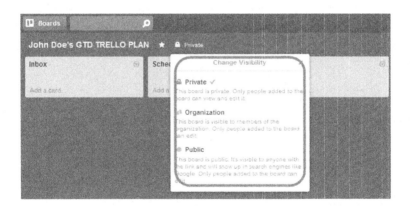

You can set the visibility to private, organization or public. A board that's on Private Mode means only users who are added as members can see and edit the board. A board on Organization Mode is visible to members of the organization, but only users added as members can edit. A Public board is visible to anyone with a link to the board. It also shows up in search engines like Google, but only users added as members can edit.

Vote and comment capabilities are available to all TRELLO members, but you can also turn these features off for public members just by going to the Settings menu.

Implementing GTD in Trello

We have finally arrived at the very core of this book which is to implement the Getting Things Done methodology with TRELLO. Your externalized thoughts from the GTD system will all be transferred to TRELLO. You don't have to worry since TRELLO's way of organizing tasks perfectly complements the GTD method.

Setting up a **TRELLO GTD** System in 30 Minutes

I will help you step by step on how you can set up the GTD method in TRELLO that will cover every aspect of your life from small projects to big goals, from family life to work life. In this chapter, there are two ways where you can implement the GTD method in TRELLO.

Let's start with the first one. First, you need to create a board. The numbered items below represent the names of the lists. Beside each item is a description of what the cards should contain..

1. *Inbox* - This is the list where you can write whatever task comes to mind. Consider it your brainstorm list. Review this list several times a week and move the cards to the context-specific list.

2. *Scheduled* - This contains a list of tasks that already have an assigned deadline or date to perform. Tasks that have a closer due date should be placed at the very top of the list.

3. *Waiting on* - This represents the tasks that you cannot do yet since they are dependent on a third party. For example, you may have to wait on someone to send you a document or make a delivery before you can do the task. These tasks may not be dependent on you, but it's still important that you keep track of them.

4. *Perhaps* - This represents the list of things you want to do but don't have the time to accomplish. A good example is a task that you keep putting off because you either lack time or resources. Consider these your extra tasks.

5. *Running* - These are the tasks that you are currently doing. This list helps you focus on the things you need to do. When you are distracted, a quick glance at the list will help you get back on track.

6. *Done* - This should contain tasks you have already finished. Nothing feels more satisfying than looking at a long list of accomplished tasks. When the list becomes too long, you can always archive the cards. Although it's no longer visible on the board, you can always refer to it later by using the website's search engine.

Your board's title can be whatever name you wish to have depending on what project or goal you are working on. If the items above were to be transferred to the board, it should look like this.

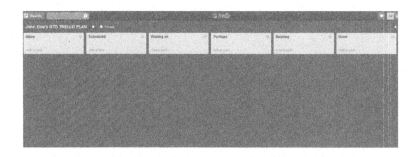

From here, you can start creating the cards for each list. If you've made a mistake of making a card in the wrong list, don't worry because the cards are easily movable. Just drag the card and move it to the right list.

Let's move on to the second way that you can set up GTD with TRELLO. Names of your lists should include the following:

1. *Big Rocks* – This contains priorities in life that you want to spend majority of your time. There's no limit to how many big rocks you want to add.

2. *Today* – This list contains the items you hope to accomplish today.

3. *Incoming* – These are the tasks that have yet to be prioritized.

4. *This Week* – These are tasks which you hope to accomplish within the week.

5. *Later* – These tasks are the ones you would like to eventually do but are not that urgent

6. *Waiting On* – These require action on another's part.

7. *Done* – These are the tasks you have accomplished today.

If you were to transfer these items to TRELLO, your board should look like this.

The same principles still apply where you need to add as many details as you can on the cards to ensure a smooth workflow. Aside from writing tasks on cards, you can also add details by clicking on the card. This is highly advisable so that you can have a clear picture of what actions you should take to finish the task.

Here, you can add details like a description of the task and objectives to be met. As the project develops, you can use the comment section to add more information that will help you accomplish the tasks faster.

As an example, I've provided a figure below on how a detailed card looks like. This is what appears when you click on the "Groceries" card under the "Scheduled" list. Under due date, I put June 25 at 5:00 PM as the deadline. In the description box, I put in "Trader Joe's right after lunch" which indicates the time and place where and when I should be doing the groceries. Underneath is a checklist named "What to buy" and beneath it is the list of things that need to be purchased. I find that making a card as detailed as possible helps make a task seem less daunting. Everything is set from the time and place down to the last item that needs to be purchased.

Here is an example of another detailed card titled "Travel to Vancouver" but this one falls under the "Waiting On" list. Let's just say that you are still waiting for a final approval from your boss, which explains why this card is still on the "Waiting On" list. You have relatives in Vancouver and there's a chance you might meet them so you decide to create a checklist of what you need to do when you see them. Encircled in red are the details of your trip to

Vancouver.

I put a sticker on the card just for added effect. These stickers do nothing more than to make your board more visually appealing. In this case, getting an approval from the boss is quite an urgent matter, which is why I decided to add a clock to the card. When you click on the card, what appears is the figure below.

Aside from the date and time of your trip to Vancouver are checklists describing the things you need to do while you are in there. There are two separate lists: one for business and one for family. It's easier to go through the day when the errands are organized separately.

Every time you create a card, a good exercise to do is to ask yourself "What information can I add?" Once you have formulated on a detail, attach it to the card by using the appropriate feature. This helps you classify a task better and helps you concentrate on a task more since all of the information is found in one reference point.

Aside from task information, you can also assign color-coded labels. You can choose from six colors which provide a better context of the tasks. It helps you distinguish tasks just by glancing at the label color. You can even add names for these labels and enable the color blind-friendly mode.

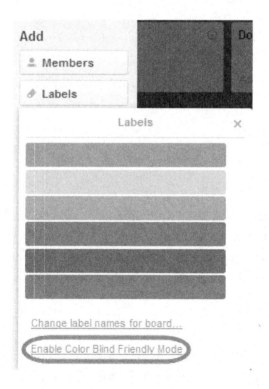

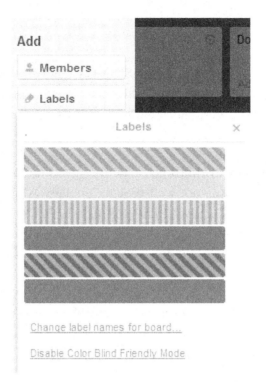

Setting up each of these TRELLO GTD systems will typically take you less than 30 minutes. Once you've finished creating the board and the lists, you can follow the time frames below for each task when implementing TRELLO GTD:

20 minutes of reviewing your board. This can be done in the morning where your mind is still fresh. Spend this time reviewing your board. Delete unnecessary tasks and change whatever needs to be modified. Pick 3-4 items which you think would make a big impact if you acted on them now and move them to the appropriate list. After that, you don't need to look at any other list except for Scheduled, Running or Today for the rest of the day.

15 minutes for brain dump. This is when you write whatever it is in your head. Put all of these ideas and thoughts in your Inbox list. Doing this proves very therapeutic as it clears your mind.

5 minutes of evaluation. Sometimes, you waste too much time on a project that was not well-thought enough. What you can do in the next 5 minutes is to evaluate it. Break down a task and see if it's really worth doing. If it's not, remove it from your list and archive or delete it.

5 minutes of creating a structural outline. You've already decided to go through a project, but you're not sure how to start it. Spend these few minutes mapping out the structure of the project. Connect things together and figure out your entry point.

15 minutes surge of work. This is for enormous projects where you can't seem to figure out where to start. Apply the 5 minute strategy above and spend your first 15 minutes working on the first task. Doing 15 minutes of uninterrupted work lessens mental stress. If you are working on a bigger project, try adding 15 more minutes. Add times in increments of 15 minutes depending on how large your project is. You can do 30 to 60 minutes. It doesn't matter as long as it's enough to get the work done.

Improving work productivity with TRELLO GTD

I just showed you how you can use the TRELLO GTD method for personal management, but what about the tasks where you need to work with other people? It's simple. Just have everyone sign up for TRELLO and you can start collaborating on a project.

Assuming you are the administrator of the board and everyone in the team is already a member, you can start assigning tasks. You are not limited to one board alone. If the scope of a project requires more boards, feel free to create more and assign members to different boards depending on where their skills are suited best.

To add a member to a card, click on the card and click on Members from the right side of the card. Type the member's name or you can also click on their avatar.

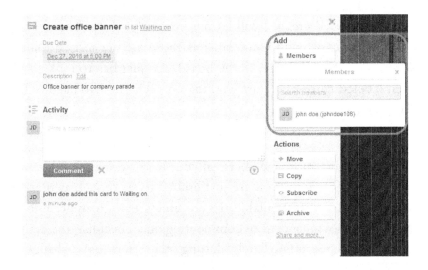

You may also drag and drop members to cards. Just view the Member's area in the right sidebar of the board, drag and drop a user's avatar directly onto the card. You will know exactly who is working on a task simply by looking whose avatar is on it.

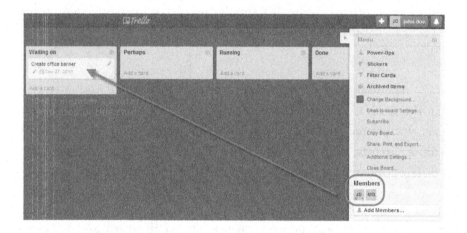

Another alternative to assigning members to a task is to give each person a color. Just like members, you can also add several colors to a task. For example, I would like my member, MG, to do all the work labeled green. I will let her know ahead that she needs to look out for cards with green label as those are her responsibilities. Now every time MG checks the board, she just has to look for the green-labeled cards and start working on each one. No need to look elsewhere.

If you have more members on your team, you can assign them with the other colors. You are just limited to six though as there are only six label colors available. Every time a team member initiates actions like moving a card or commenting on a checklist, the activity feed gets updated immediately alerting other users that a change has just been made.

Advanced Tips and tricks when using TRELLO GTD

Once you've mastered TRELLO, you can move on to learning techniques that will help you become more efficient. In this portion, I'll teach you a few techniques in using TRELLO GTD. TRELLO seems simple when used the for the first time since it's all just a series of lists, but underneath the boards and lists are features that you can take advantage of, to get the job done faster.

Let's start with the keyboard shortcuts. You will be amazed at the things you can do at TRELLO with just a push of a button. Below is a table of the complete keyboard shortcuts. Try using these shortcuts when you're in TRELLO.

Keyboard Shortcut	Action
← ↓ / J ↑ / K →	The arrows let you navigate the cards to their respective directions. Pressing "J" will select the card below the current card while pressing "K" will select the card above the current card.
B	Opens the boards menu. You can then search and navigate for boards with the up

	and down arrows. Pressing enter with a board selected will open it.
/	Puts the cursor in the search box in the header.
C	Archives a card.
D	Open the due date picker for a card.
E	Hover on a card and press E. This will open a quick edit mode which lets you edit the card attributes like title and due date.
Esc	Closes an open dialog window or pop-over or cancel edits and comments you're composing.
Enter	Opens a currently selected card.
F	Opens the card filter menu and the search by title input is automatically focused.
L	Opens a pop-over of the available labels. Clicking a label then add or remove it from the card. Pressing the following number keys, will apply or remove that label: 1 – Green 2 – Yellow 3 – Orange 4 – Red 5 – Purple 6 - Blue
M	Opens the Add/Remove members

	menu. Assign or un-assign a member by clicking on their avatar.
N	Opens a pop-over allowing you to add a card after a currently selected card.
<>	Moves a card to the adjacent left or right list.
Q	Toggles "card assigned to me" filter.
S	Subscribes or unsubscribes you from a card. Subscribing to a card gives you notifications for most actions to that card.
Space	Assigns or un-assigns you to a card.
T	Edits the title when viewing a card. When the cursor is hovered over a card, pressing "T" will open the card and edit the title.
V	Adds or removes your vote on a card.
W	Collapse And expands the board sidebar.
X	Clears all active card filters.
?	Opens the shortcuts page.
#	When adding a new card, just type "#" plus label's color or title and get a list of matching labels. You can then use the up and down arrows to navigate the resulting list. Press the "Enter" or "Tab" button lets you add the label to the composed card. Labels will be added to the card when you submit.
^	When adding a new card, type "^" plus

	a list name or position in a list. Type "top" or "bottom" to add to the top or bottom of the current list. You can use the up and down arrows to navigate the resulting list. Pressing enter or tab automatically changes the position of the composed card.

Below are more advanced techniques you can use at TRELLO.

Double-click any free space on the board

Doing this lets you open a new list. By default, the list will automatically go at the top right at the same column where you created the list.

Drag, drop and paste attachments

Instead of opening a folder, you can just drag and drop files from your desktop to TRELLO and upload them. You can also drag images from other websites directly to cards.

You can also do the copy and paste option. Paste images by right-clicking on the image and select Copy Image. Go back to your card, open it, or hover over a card and press "command + v" for Mac or "control + v" for windows. Unfortunately, this copy-paste option only works in Chrome, but this feature will soon be supported by other browsers.

Copy boards, lists, cards and checklists

Do you have a board or a list you want to use as a template? For boards, all you need to do is click on Options and select Copy Board. For lists, click the menu found on the upper right corner of a list and select copy List. For a card, just open the desired card and under Actions, select Copy. You can even copy checklist items from other checklists by creating a new checklist and selecting Copy Items From.

For copying boards:

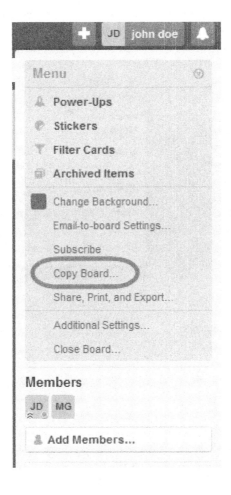

For copying lists:

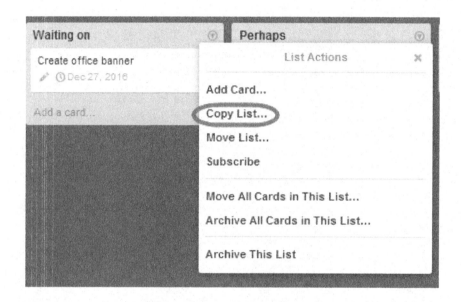

For copying cards:

For copying checklists:

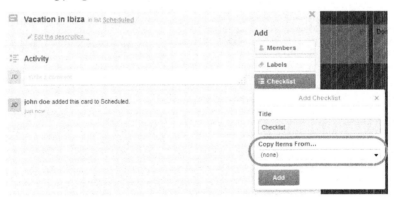

Drag board to scroll

TRELLO lists are arranged horizontally and sometimes, it can be a pain to look for a list when you have to scroll horizontally with the scroll bar. TRELLO has made it easy to navigate your board with the capability to click anywhere on the board, just hold and it will let you drag the board left and right.

Archive lists in bulk

Want to archive all the cards in the list but not delete the list just yet? You can archive all the lists in bulk by clicking the menu on the top right corner and select Archive All Cards in This List.

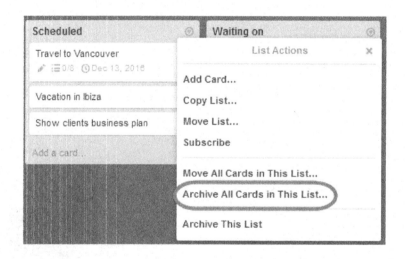

Using Power-Ups

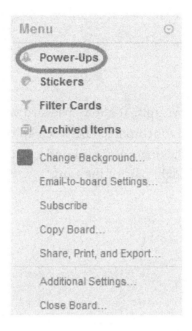

Another feature that some TRELLO users might not know about is the Power-Ups option. You can find this on the Menu board. When you click on it, you will get three advanced features called Voting, Calendar and Card Aging. Power-ups are enabled by the board and you can disable each one if you don't need to use it any longer.

Voting is a power-up that allows users to vote on the cards. The votes are stored and synchronized between all users using the board. You can vote by clicking on a card and click on the Vote button found on the lower right part of the card.

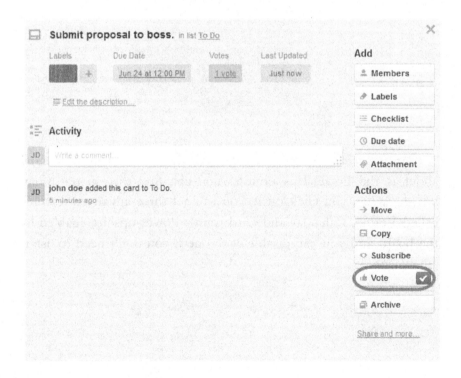

People who can vote on a card will depend on your board's permission level. This feature is great when there is a task where you need to get everyone's consensus.

Card aging is exactly what the feature's name implies. A card visibly ages as time passes indicating that there hasn't been any activity for quite some time. As time passes, the cards become progressively more transparent. The card's aging thresholds are 1, 2 and 4 weeks. If a card has a new activity, the age counter resets and it will look new again. Regular mode makes an aging card look transparent while Pirate mode causes the cards turn yellow, crack and tear like an old treasure map. This is great for reminding you of tasks you haven't checked in a while. It is also a way to determine whether a task is worth doing. If it's been there for quite a long time, then it's probably not important.

The Calendar power-up lets you view TRELLO in calendar mode. This feature is very useful for time-sensitive tasks and projects with multiple due-dates. By clicking on the Calendar button, you immediately get a calendar view of your tasks arranged according to due date.

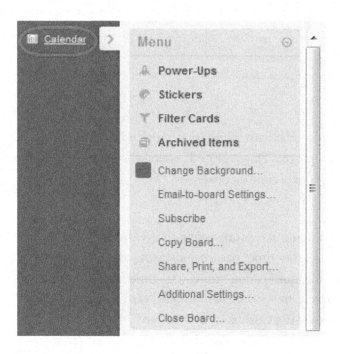

The figure below is how TRELLO looks like. The cards are arranged according to due date. You can easily drag and drop the cards to different calendar days if you wish to change the due date. Click on each calendar day to expand your view of the tasks for the day.

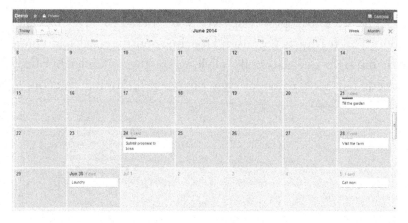

If you have the iCalendar app, you can export your TRELLO card's information by going back to the Power-ups option. Look for Settings and just copy the URL for your iCalendar feed. Log on to your iCal and paste the URL. Doing this automatically copies all of your tasks' due dates to iCalendar.

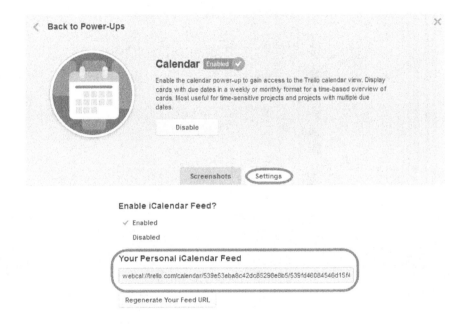

Filter cards make searching easier

If you have an extensive list of cards on your board where it can take a few minutes to look for a task, you can use the Filter option found on the Menu. This option lets you look for items by label, or by due date. If you want to be more specific, you can filter by term by typing it in the search bar.

Use stickers

Stickers are an extra feature of TRELLO that you can use to make your board more visually appealing. They are not really that important, but you can use them for added detail. The stickers below are available in the free version. If you upgrade, you get the Taco

68

Pack, Pete the Computer, and other customer stickers.

This option can be found on the Menu on the upper right corner of the board. You can move a sticker from one card to another by dragging and you can remove it by hovering on the sticker, press E, click on the sticker and select Remove.

Visualizing your to-do list with TRELLO

Most people use To-do lists to keep track of tasks they need to do. These lists can vary from person to person. Some people keep multiple to-do lists to compartmentalize different areas of their life: family, work and personal development among other things. Others prefer to keep just one list that has everything in it.

Although keeping many lists is a good way to be organized, it can sometimes get confusing. You have to carry these lists with you all the time to make sure you are on track with everything. The same also applies to just having one list. The tasks on the list will eventually grow overtime and sometimes important tasks get into the backburner simply because they are already at the bottom part of the list.

To avoid these kinds of setbacks, I highly suggest you visualize your to-do list using TRELLO. Not only does it keep your tasks organized, it also makes tasks that need to be prioritized easier to find.

Here, I'll show you how to make your to-do list work with TRELLO. We'll start by creating the first board named "This Week's Projects." It will be your go-to board and it should consist of four lists namely:

1. **On deck** consists of tasks you want to accomplish in a particular week. You can fill this list at the start of the week. This will also be the list where you will base your daily to-do list.

2. **Today** consists of to-do items you want to accomplish that day. Build this list the night before by using the tasks on the On Deck list.

3. **Waiting For/On hold** should consist of tasks from On Deck or Today that you are not working on actively. It's either because you have no control over it or you simply just decided to put off the task for some reason.

4. **All done** are tasks you have already completed. Instead of crossing off a task, you move it from your to-do list to this list. You can move the cards around the same time that you're also building next week's lists.

Here is how your visualized to-do list should look like.

Now it's time to create a second board. This should be named "Big Picture." This board should consist of lists for projects you're working for both personal and professional. For each project, you can then start cards for each actionable task. Each week, when you're making your On Deck list, refer to your Big Picture Board and use the card's Move option to send the cards to This Week's Projects Board.

Your "Big Picture" board can look like this:

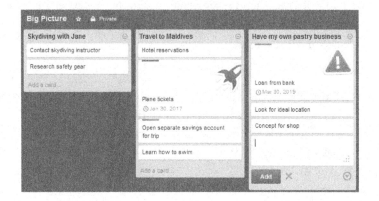

The lists consist of big goals that are yet to be accomplished. If you find a task that you can do within the week transfer the card to the "This Week's Project" board.

Arranging your tasks this way allows you to separate the big tasks from the small ones. Your dreams are slowly realized as you move cards from the "Big Picture" list each week.

Attaching documents from Google Drive

TRELLO gives you the ability to attach documents from a card directly from Google Drive. Click on Attachment and choose Google Drive. Files attached from the drive will open Google Drive in a new window. It can be edited, saved and doesn't have to be reattached to the TRELLO card.

When a user has multiple Google accounts, sometimes the form that loads in TRELLO is the incorrect account. In order to get the file you need to have attached, you need to make sure that you are signed in on the right Google account. To solve this issue, you can go to *https://drive.google.com* and switch accounts. If it still does not work, you will have to log out all of your Google accounts and then log back in to the Google account you need to access.

TRELLO Tennis

With TRELLO Tennis, you will need to make two important columns namely:

- *Ball in my court* - projects which require you to do something. You can name this column "My court."
- *Ball in their court* - projects which require you to wait for someone else to do something, for example, approve a topic, provide feedback on a document, and reply to an email. You can name this column "Their court."

Your goal each day is to move projects from the "My court" column to the "Their court" column. I recommend that you regularly review the "My court" column and place the most urgent items on top. You should also check on the "Their court" column in case you need to follow up or offer assistance.

TRELLO GTD as A Multi-Purpose System

I've mentioned earlier that TRELLO can be used in different workflows. In this chapter, I'll show you how to use TRELLO GTD in different aspects of your life. It doesn't matter if you are still a student or an office employee, whether you are single or you have a family. TRELLO is a tool that will help you keep your life together and get the tasks done right away.

Before we get started, I want to give a disclosure that the boards I have below are just examples. You don't have to strictly follow them if they don't fit the nature of your tasks. TRELLO is a very flexible tool and you can always apply the GTD methodology by categorizing your lists however you desire.

Getting Things Done With TRELLO

At work

When you're using TRELLO GTD at work, you can use it in two ways, either by yourself or with a group. I would recommend you maintain these two boards so you can keep track of your solo responsibilities and your assigned tasks in the group. You can name the first board "My Work" and the other as "Group work." Naming the second board depends on who the administrator of the board is.

Under "My Work," you can create a modified list, which includes Inbox, Later, Waiting, This Week, Today, and Done. The "Inbox" contains all of the ideas that come out of your head, which you will process and transfer later onto the other lists. Later are the tasks that are not that urgent. Think of it as tasks that you will only do if you are in the mood. "Waiting" lists are the tasks where you have to wait on someone else before you can accomplish a task. It can also serve as a reminder of who you need to follow up with. "This Week" list are tasks for the week. These are the tasks that need to be done by the end of the week but not due today. "Today" lists are tasks for today. If it's on the list, then you need to do it immediately. The "Done" list consists of cards with the tasks you've already accomplished. This should be a long list by the end of the week.

The board should look like this.

If you are currently working on a confidential project or task, you can opt to make your board Private where only you can see it. If your project requires the supervision of a colleague or your boss, you can always change the privacy settings. Every board has a link so if you want to invite anyone you want to participate, just send them the URL to the board. Whenever there's a change, everyone else can see it right away either through the activity feed or by email notification.

For group work, it depends on the type of project you are working on. There really is no perfect kind of board template since projects can vary. Typically, groups who use TRELLO name their lists using the three basic stages of a project, namely Planning, In Progress and Deployment Ready.

Depending on which members are assigned to a card, only they have the capability to move it to another list when appropriate. There might be times when members are too immersed in their work that they cannot be bothered to move the cards. I suggest that you brief your members ahead before using TRELLO. Have them inform you every time a task on a card is accomplished so that you can move it to the appropriate list. Only you should have this capability to avoid any confusion on who should move the card.

Since you can access TRELLO using any device, I recommend you to use the board during conference meetings where you can have a clear view of where your project stands and what each member's remaining tasks are. This saves a lot of time from you having to make PowerPoint presentations.

I also just wanted to share with you another strategy when you are working with a team. Instead of naming the lists according to project stage, you can name them according to each member instead. Here is an example.

Now that each team member has their own list, it's time to create cards for each person that contains their corresponding tasks.

One reason why this strategy works so well is because it's clear to the members what their responsibilities are. Just by looking at the board, they know exactly what aspects of the project they should be working on. They don't have to look elsewhere but their own lists. Once a task is done, you can then just have the members archive the cards. If you're the administrator of the board, you can set deadlines by creating due dates for cards that are urgent. You can also encourage your members to assign due dates for their not-so urgent tasks. This helps create a responsible mindset towards tasks.

At school

Using TRELLO GTD at work is almost the same as using it if you were at work. You can either utilize it to manage your own schoolwork or you can organize group projects with it. Let's start first by using TRELLO to manage your semester's subject loads. It can feel overwhelming sometimes when your assignment notebook is filled with many notes on assignments from different subjects. You have to flip the pages back and forth to review which subject assignment is almost due. As a way to organize your assignments and study materials, you can create a TRELLO board for every semester.

I created a board below and named it SY 2014-2015 to indicate what school year the board is for. Each subject has its own card. You can refer to this board by the end of the day. You can then create a new card for whatever task was assigned to you on that day and make sure to indicate a deadline set by the teacher and add more details if you can.

The number of lists you create will depend on how many subjects you have on that certain semester. After making a list for each subject, you should create one more list named Complete where you can move cards for tasks which you've already finished. Once the semester is over, you can archive the list and fill it up with new tasks for the new semester.

Let's say you were tasked by your English professor to write a literary criticism on Edgar Allan Poe's The Raven. Its deadline is on November 27, 2014, 1:00 PM. so you indicate that deadline on the card. You also just attached a file to the card related to the report. You're going to need that as a reference in your report later.

Here is an example of how the card should look like.

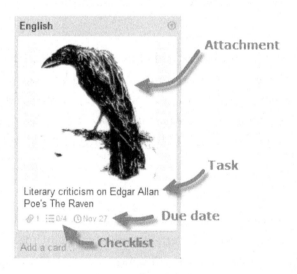

Indicated beside the due date is a checklist with four items on it. By clicking the card, you will see the items on the checklist as well as other details.

Literary criticism on Edgar Allan Poe's The Raven in list English

Due Date

Nov 27 at 1:00 PM

✎ Edit the description...

Attachments

raven.gif
Added 14 minutes ago
⬇ Download ⬜ Remove Cover ✕ Delete

Add an attachment...

Report structure
0%

☐ Introduction
☐ Body
☐ Supporting points
☐ Conclusion

Add item

Add

👤 Members
🏷 Labels
☰ Checklist
🕐 Due date
📎 Attachment

Actions

➔ Move
🗐 Copy
◯ Subscribe
🗄 Archive

Share and more...

The checklist consists of the parts of the literary criticism. This is to help make the writing easier. The list includes an introduction, body, supporting points, and a conclusion.

Assignments are not the only tasks you can add to the lists. It's also great for reports and required readings. The Attachment option is going to be highly useful for school as you don't need to write down all important notes on an index card. You just have to attach a photo, a screenshot of a webpage of a PDF file. It's like digitalizing your index cards. After you are done with an assignment, just archive it. By the end of the semester, you will have yourself an information-rich archive you can refer to it later when you are assigned a similar study in the future.

You can do the same for your other projects. Take advantage of the checklists for a smoother workflow. The example above is just a basic example. If you need to create more checklists to help organize your task, then by all means, do so.

Now how about if you're working with a group? Let's say your Chemistry teacher assigned you to do an investigative project together with two other people in the class. This project can be difficult to manage, especially if the three of you have different schedules. You'll rarely get anything done if there's little time in the day where the three of you are available. This is where TRELLO GTD can be very useful. You will be collaborating on the project without needing each other's physical presence. The free time you share can be used to discuss and finalize important things about the project.

What you need to do first is to assign a leader. The leader will be the one to create the board and add the members. Once the board is created, you can start creating lists that define the stages of your group project development. You can apply this strategy or use the one I showed above where I created a list for each team member. It depends on which of the two strategies your members are comfortable using.

Once you start working in TRELLO, you don't have to constantly worry about finding the time to meet with each other. As long as you have a computer, a tablet or a mobile device and an internet connection, you can do your project anywhere. You can give updates to your group mates by simply mentioning them in the comments or referring them to the newsfeed. If there's a file that you think might be helpful for the project, you can attach it on the appropriate card and it'll be visible to your group mates. You can even add comments and write what you think of it.

At home: groceries and meal planning

TRELLO GTD is not only great for business and projects. You can also use it to organize your home. In this part, we will tackle tasks that take up a huge chunk of the housework: doing the groceries and planning meals.

I will give you an example of how you can use TRELLO GTD for your groceries. You need to create a new board first and name it Groceries. For the lists, you can create them by month and make cards for each week. Here is how it looks like.

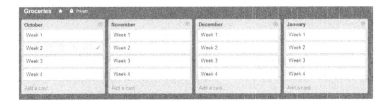

Click on October's Week 1 and let's see what we need to pick up at the groceries for that week.

Under Week 1 card is a checklist named Masterlist. For every week, you will need to create this kind of checklist to indicate the items that you need to pick up at the grocery. At the start of the week, you can start filling out this checklist of the things that you need. I would suggest you fill this list after you've checked your pantry stock. This will give you an idea of what supplies are almost out.

As soon as you've finalized the list, just take your phone with you and once you arrive at the grocery, you can just access TRELLO from there. You'll save a lot of time and money since you already know what you need to buy. You don't have to wander around the store aimlessly picking items you don't really need.

If you want to take organized grocery shopping to the next level, you can create separate checklists for each grocery category. Here is an example.

In the example above, I made Week 2's checklists very specific. There is a separate list for toiletries, meat and fruits. Doing this helps you avoid jumping from one grocery aisle to another. As you walk through the grocery to pick the items you need, tick each one from the list. You'll have a satisfying feeling after seeing the blue bar move until the list is 100% complete.

If you're too busy to do the groceries, you can have someone else do it for you. It can be your spouse or your roommate. No need to enumerate that long list of things you need them to buy for you. Just refer them to the board and the checklist. You might just make grocery shopping an enjoyable experience for them once they use TRELLO GTD.

Bonus tip: I know there are instances when you suddenly remember needing to buy an important item, but you can't access TRELLO at the moment. It would also be a hassle to access the website from time to time to add items that you need. I suggest you keep a digital list. Nothing complicated. It can be Microsoft word or a note app on your phone. Since I'm using the computer most of the time, I take my notes using Sticky Notes. It's very convenient since it's the very first and last thing I see whenever I use turn on or shut down my computer. Whenever there's an item I remember buying, I just write it on a Sticky Note. Here is an example.

eggs

bacon

canned tuna

kale

broccoli

As soon as you're able to access TRELLO, you can then copy this list onto your card's checklist. Now here's the cool part. You actually don't need to copy and paste each item. You just have to select and copy everything from your digital list, then go to TRELLO and paste it on your chosen checklist.

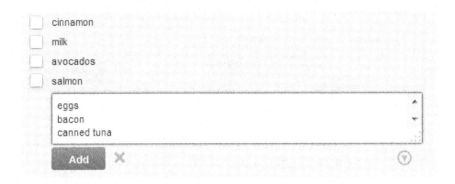

Clicks Add and TRELLO automatically makes the checklist for you.

What I just showed you is an example of how you can create a grocery list using the TRELLO GTD method. I have another example of how you can organize your grocery list. Here is how it looks like.

Instead of arranging the grocery items by month and week, I created a list for each type of item. In this board, you'll see there's a list for produce, meat and toiletries. On each card are the names of the items you need to buy. The last list is named In Stock. Every time you buy the items, you just have to move the cards to the In Stock List. This way, you'll know what's in stock at your pantry. When the supply runs out, you can always drag the card back to the list it belongs to.

What's great about this method is that it lets you see the items clearly. You don't need to click on the card for more details since the item's name is already indicated as the card's name. You also don't have to write down the items repeatedly. You just have to move a card to its designated list if you run out of stock of it in your pantry.

Now let's talk about meal planning. If you live in a big household, meal planning is very important. You have to make sure you get the right amount of items that is enough for everybody. TRELLO GTD can help make this possible for you.

You can start by referring to the second grocery list I made earlier. This one:

Beside the In Stock list, you can create another list named Meals. After doing your groceries, you can start planning your meals for the week. Check the In Stock list and see what recipes you can make with the ingredients available listed in the In Stock list. In the Meals list above, I came up with meals that can be prepared with the items available.

The Meal list should typically have 21 cards assuming that you eat 3 times a day in a week. The labels will be useful in this part. To distinguish which meals are which, I decided to label breakfasts, lunches and dinners by color. Violet labels are for breakfast, yellow for lunch and red for dinner. You can also attach recipes to the cards with meals you don't know how to make. Once the week is over, you can archive cards in bulk and create a whole new plan for the coming week.

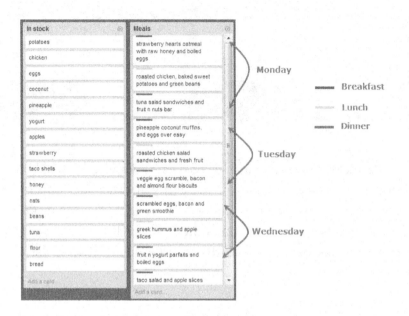

This method of planning your meals is best because everything is set for the week. You don't have to spend time staring at your pantry stock trying to decide what meal to prepare. If you're the health-conscious type, this is also an amazing way to maintain your healthy lifestyle. You get to track down the meals you've had and if you want to eat the same meal again, just go to the Board Menu, click Archived Items and you'll see a complete list of meals you've eaten.

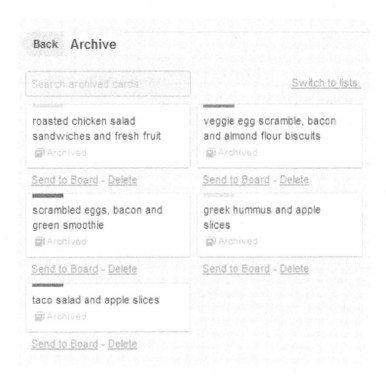

If you're looking at your archives and notice that your meals are getting repetitive, you can just mix things up by creating new recipes.

Aside from meal planning, TRELLO can also be used for other household activities like chores, barbecue Sundays and weekend projects. For a comprehensive board on your household, you can make three lists: Cleaning Tasks, Mails and Bills and Personal Projects. The Cleaning Tasks list focuses on the specific areas of the house that need to be cleaned. Mails and Bills are more crucial since they typically involve money. Personal projects are lower priority than the Mails and Bills list. It's important you set due dates for cards under this list. Each person in the house has a designated label color. For example, cleaning the garage requires two people so you need to put two label colors on the card indicating the people that you want to assign the task to.

91

The board's lists can also be named according to each person's name in the household. Under each list contains the cards with their responsibilities. This is a great way to develop accountability on each person in the household. No need to worry about accessibility since TRELLO is supported by all browsers and anyone can just look up the board to see what their tasks for the day are.

When you experiment with TRELLO's features, you will see that it's not only working well for business projects alone. It's a great management tool that you can apply with whatever household that needs to be organized.

For your small business

It's a given that when you run a business, you will manage people. As an entrepreneur, you can organize your business by creating a TRELLO board that's easily accessible to your employees. Have them enroll for the service and invite them to your board. You can organize the lists by employee name, progress or importance. It's really up to you. Business comes in different forms so it's best to modify your board according to your business' unique aspects. Remember, one kind of board may work for one business but not for another. I will show you some examples on how you can utilize TRELLO GTD in running your business.

If you plan on making lists by employee name, you can apply the strategy discussed earlier. Every person has a swim lane with their individual tasks written on their cards. Your responsibility as a leader is to track each employee's progress. Set due dates for important tasks. You can make it a special rule to have your employee label a card yellow if they're currently working on it and green if the task is already finished.

There are instances where members might get confused on who should move the card. To avoid this, let your members know that only you will move the cards. You will know if it is time to move the card just by looking at the label color.

Any feedback or suggestion you may have on a task, you can just write it in the comment box and tag a member by mentioning them. This will bring their attention to the card and inform them of how they should do a task.

Another way to utilize TRELLO GTD in your business is to categorize lists by priority. Doing this helps your employees stay on track with the tasks that need to be accomplished immediately. Here's an example of how it looks like. I still used the same business example, but the lists are different as they are named according to priority.

If you are working with a group of six people or less, you can use the six label colors for each person. All of your employees will automatically know what their responsibilities are just by looking at the card's labels. You can also add as many as six labels on each card. It all depends on how many people need to work on a certain task. In the example above, I assigned one person who is good at writing to make the press release. The website heading is a bit challenging, so I decided to put two labels indicating the two people from the team who are knowledgeable in graphic design and web development to work on the task. If there are any relevant files that need to be added, you can have your employees upload the files directly from Dropbox or Google Drive.

Running a business efficiently doesn't have to cost you a lot. TRELLO is a free tool and when you apply the GTD method, you'll accomplish great feats in your business. It will not only benefit you, but also your business and your employees.

For authors

The TRELLO GTD method is perfect for authors since it requires writing down all ideas and have them organized into lists. You know how terrible it is to have a surge of ideas and then lose them later all because you didn't bother to take notes. One of the main principles of the GTD method is to externalize your ideas. As an author, you should apply this method in your daily life and utilize TRELLO to organize your thoughts.

I suggest that you always bring with you a pen and paper everywhere you go. Inspiration can strike at the most unexpected moments and you want to make sure you can record all those ideas. You can then transfer these written ideas later when you open your TRELLO board.

You can start by creating a TRELLO board with individual lists for ideas, chapter outlines, character development, works in progress and completed chapters. Here's how it looks like.

Whatever is in your notes will go directly to the Ideas list. As you write, just move the ideas to the appropriate list and fill it with information that will help put your book together.

There are writers who just go with the flow and create stories as they write and when they finish the book, they just read through it and make the appropriate changes. And then there are those writers who prefer to organize their thoughts before they begin to write. This is where you can use the Chapter Outlines list. Create a card for each chapter. For each chapter, you can create a checklist containing the parts. If there's a part of the book that needs to be fact-checked, you can attach documents and research materials using the Attachment option.

You can even add other members to your board. This happens only if you are comfortable with other people looking at your work in progress. You can add your friends and your family. You can invite your editor or your mentor to check your work and provide feedback. Let them use the comment section as an outlet to write what they think of your current work. There's no harm in getting a little constructive criticism.

If you'll be working with a group of authors on a big book project, you can collaborate with other writers by creating separate boards for different aspects of writing the book. Let's say you're working on a book about science that requires the contribution of authorities in the field. There should be separate boards for Hypothesis and Brain Storming. On each board, each author has his own list containing the ideas and hypotheses related to the project. Another board should be named Research and Experimental Information which should contain data that supports the hypothesis. Got relevant information for the project? You can just attach the file to the card and you don't have to scramble for that information in your inbox later.

TRELLO GTD can help organize your project as a whole while still giving each author the opportunity to contribute. The above paragraph is just an example of how you can utilize the tool to organize a big project. The same strategy might not apply to other kinds of books.

The system is also works great for freelance writers. It can get confusing when you're working on multiple projects for different clients. The quality of your writing is affected due to lack of focus. To avoid this, you can organize your TRELLO board by client, priority or by project. It's also advisable to keep a separate list for all of your ideas. This is similar to the Inbox list discussed earlier, where you get to write down everything that comes to mind.

Doing this gives clarity to your projects, allowing you to work on each task immediately. When you can finish a task efficiently, you can take on more work from clients which can be very beneficial to your freelance career.

Conclusion

After applying the principles you have learned in this book, being too busy or distracted will become the least of your problems. When you write everything down and organize them into lists, tasks become easier to accomplish and big goals are not as daunting anymore. Since you get tasks easily done, you have room to do more work. And more work reaps more rewards.

Yes, you may have to frequently review your lists, but this is only for you to be reassured of your situation. The goal is to review your list until you are free from having to remember everything. You never have to feel guilty about letting anything fall behind since everything is in your TRELLO GTD system. When you have an external system that you can trust to remember your tasks, like TRELLO GTD, you will feel less stressed and more relaxed.

The amazing thing about TRELLO GTD is it's a forgiving system. Results depend on how well you implement the system in your life. It can be easy to fall off from your responsibilities, but it's also easy to get back on track. The system is only as smart as you are. If you expect returns, you need to have the discipline and initiative to take action on your plans.

ABOUT DOMINIC WOLFF

Dominic Wolff is a business owner and traveller (or as he likes to call it, a globe trotter). A native from Idaho, he became interested in the mechanics of business from a very young age. From those early days of selling candy bars to running a multi-state company today, he has always been on the lookout for systems that would improve his productivity and allow him more free time to enjoy his hobbies. He frequently writes articles about personal productivity for business publications.

He believes that having a structure in place for work and life can mean the difference between being in control and merely coping.

An avid collector of fine red wines, he also owns a small wine boutique stocking only the finest of Washington, Oregon and Idaho wines. During his travels to far and wonderful places he also searches for the absolute best Zinfandel that can rival those of California. He lives in Wyoming with his wife Sarah, two German Shepherds and a tiny vineyard of his own.

BOOKS BY DOMINIC WOLFF

Master Getting Things Done the David Allen Way with Evernote

Getting Things Done (GTD) + Evernote = Ultimate Productivity

Total Time Mastery with Evernote

Your Killer Linkedin Profile

Building Connections 2014

Time Management Mastery

Speak Up!

How to Get Things Done with OneNote

One Last Thing...

Thank you so much for reading my book. I hope you really liked it. As you probably know, many people look at the reviews on Amazon before they decide to purchase a book. If you liked the book, could you please take a minute to leave a review with your feedback? 60 seconds is all I'm asking for, and it would mean the world to me.

Dominic Wolff

ORGANIZED LIVING
P R E S S

Atlanta, Georgia USA

CPSIA information can be obtained
at www.ICGtesting.com
Printed in the USA
FSOW04n0827201016
26362FS